An insect friendly garden

Arty says that insects are really important for all ecosystems. They aerate the soil, pollinate blossoms, and control insect and plant pests. Some, like beetles, are scavengers feeding on dead animals and fallen trees. They recycle nutrients back into the soil.

- 🐞 Stop using pesticides.

- 🦋 Have plants that attract insects. Make your garden as diverse as possible to attract different types of insects.

- 🐜 Plan your garden to have flowers all year.

- 🐞 Find plants that flower at night for night insects.

- 🐛 Plant lots of native plants as they will be the ones insects like.

- 🐞 Plant herbs because insects love them.

- 🐛 Make a deadwood pile in the garden for beetles.

- 🐛 Let your old vegetables go to seed.

- 🕷 Give insects some water and a place to drink. A birdbath is a good idea. Bees love drinking!

- 🦟 Make a compost heap and leave some garden areas untidy!

Here are some important things you can do to help the insect population.

My insect notebook
back cover

Become an insect detective and make a special notebook to record your finds. First, copy or scan this page to make the front and back covers. Then, on the next page you will find a sheet for recording all the insects you find. Scan or photocopy and cut each page in half. Put the sheets inside the covers and staple the whole lot together down one edge to make a notebook. Colour the covers and you are ready to go!

On each page of your notebook you have to say what type of insect you saw, the date and time you saw it and the place where you found it. In the space below your notes you can draw a sketch of the insect.

How many different insects can you find to record in your notebook? Share your favourite pages with us by :
Email at: bonjour@lespuces.co.uk
Facebook at: https://www.facebook.com/LesPucesLtd/

www.lespuces.co.uk

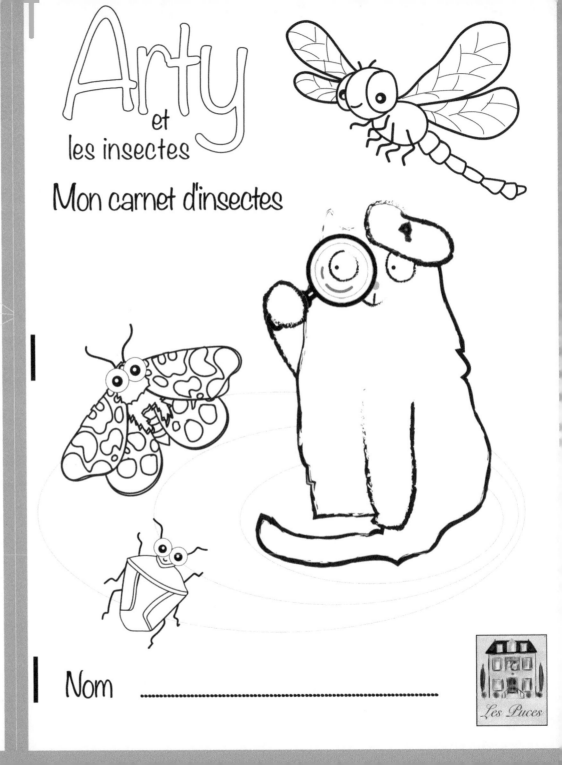

Arty
et
les insectes

Mon carnet d'insectes

Nom ....

Les Puces

Insecte

Date et l'heure

Endroit

Un Croquis

Insecte

Date et l'heure

Endroit

Un Croquis

Umbrella detective project:

There are thousands of insects all around us, so it should be easy to fill up your insect notebook with examples. One good idea for finding lots of insects is to use an umbrella! Take your umbrella and put it up. Hold it upside down under a branch or a bush and shake the branch/bush carefully. Insects should fall out into your upturned umbrella. You can use your magnifying glass to look at them and make notes. When you have finished empty the insects carefully onto the ground beside the branch/bush.

La tipule
The crane fly

Crane fly facts:

★ Crane flies look like big mosquitoes but do not bite!

★ There are about 15,000 different types of crane flies making them the largest group of flies in the world.

★ Crane flies only live for about 15 days as a fly, but spend most of their life as a lava called a 'leatherjacket' that eats grass roots!

★ Adult crane flies have very long thin legs that break easily. This may help them get away from birds if they get caught.

★ Some species of crane fly can grow up to 10 cms long!

★ Crane flies can't fly very well and are often seen wobbling in flight.

★ Crane flies have no mouth so don't actually ever eat!

Parts of an insect

All insects have three main body parts: head, thorax and abdomen. They then have other parts attached to these three segments, such as eyes, antenna and six legs. If you find a creature and it has these three main body parts and six legs then it's an insect!

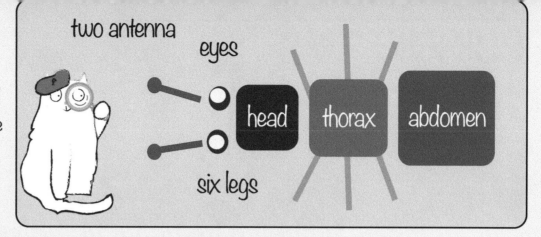

two antenna

eyes

head   thorax   abdomen

six legs

Use the two spaces below to play the game. You can copy the page or use any scraps of paper to play.

PLAYER ONE

DRAW AN INSECT GAME

Each player takes it in turn to roll a dice. You then draw the body part you rolled. The first person to complete their insect is the winner (all 13 parts). You have to start by rolling a six for a thorax and you can only draw on a body part if it connects to the parts you have already drawn. ie. you must have head to draw eyes and antenna.

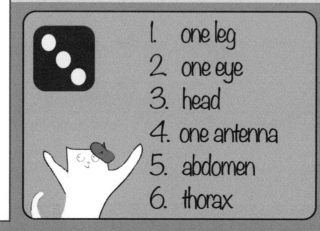

1. one leg
2. one eye
3. head
4. one antenna
5. abdomen
6. thorax

PLAYER TWO

La coccinelle

Find the ladybirds

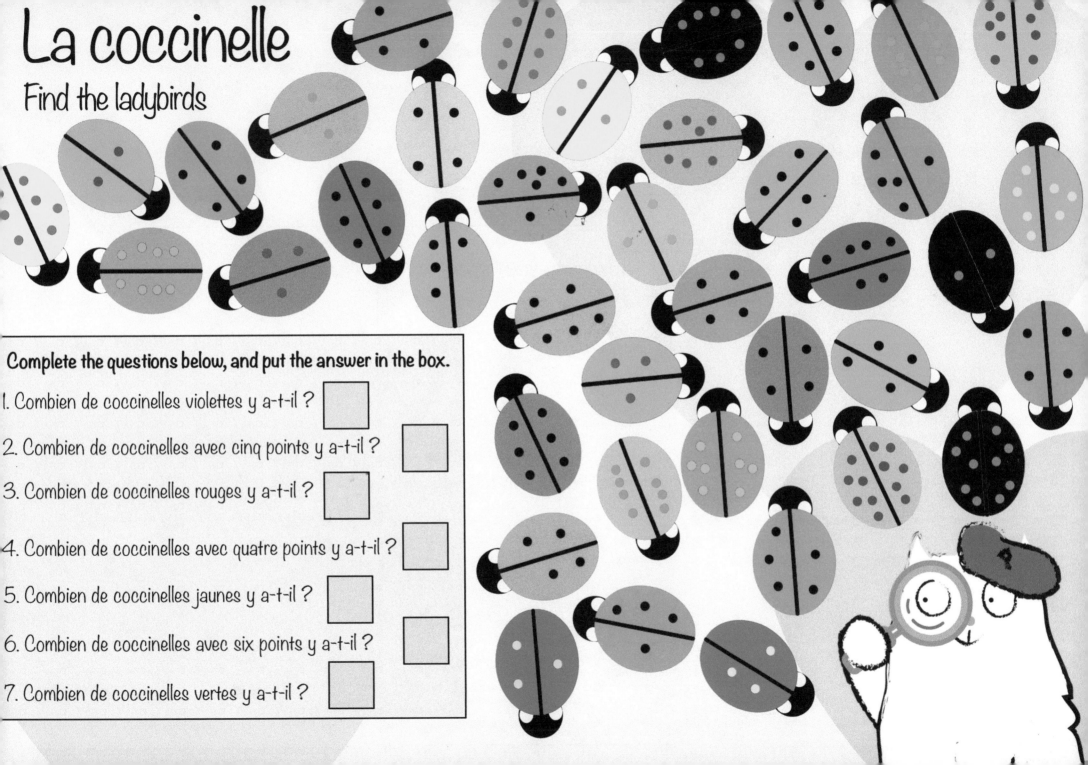

Complete the questions below, and put the answer in the box.

1. Combien de coccinelles violettes y a-t-il ?

2. Combien de coccinelles avec cinq points y a-t-il ?

3. Combien de coccinelles rouges y a-t-il ?

4. Combien de coccinelles avec quatre points y a-t-il ?

5. Combien de coccinelles jaunes y a-t-il ?

6. Combien de coccinelles avec six points y a-t-il ?

7. Combien de coccinelles vertes y a-t-il ?

Colouring page

Arty says "get colouring!"

Combien ?

How many?

Count how many of each insect you can find in the picture and write the number in the correct box. You should count in French of course!

8	80 180 ₇₈ₒ	8 3	14	5 7	11
la coccinelle	l'abeille	le papillon	la libellule	le syrphe	le papillon de nuit

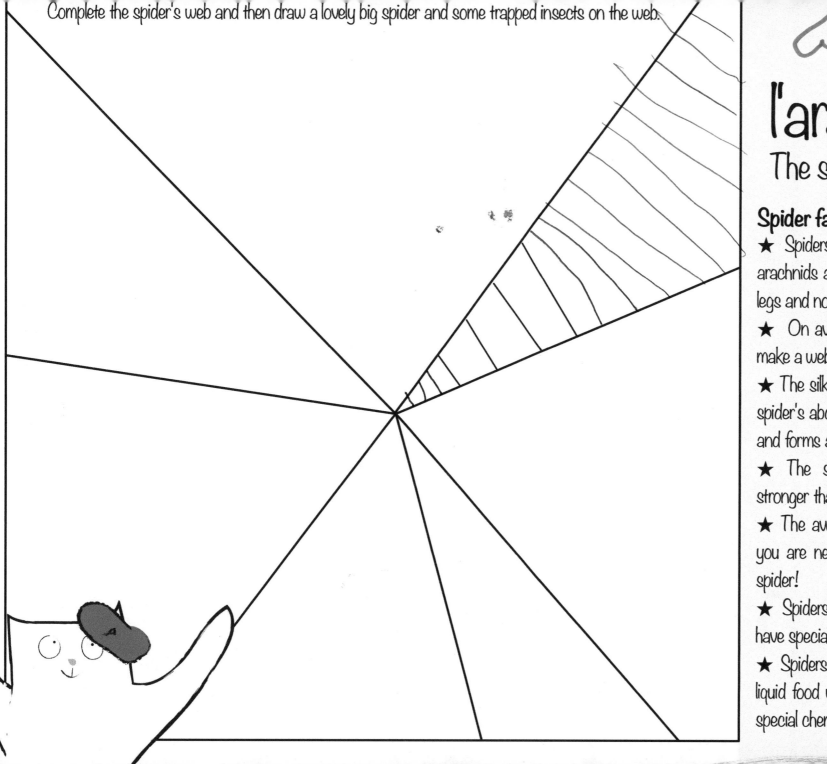

Complete the spider's web and then draw a lovely big spider and some trapped insects on the web.

l'araignée
The spider

Spider facts:

★ Spiders are not actually insects. They are arachnids as they have two body segments, eight legs and no antenna!

★ On average it takes a spider 60 minutes to make a web, and some make a new one each day!

★ The silk for a web is actually a liquid inside the spider's abdomen. When released it becomes solid and forms a web.

★ The spider's silk strands are five times stronger than steel.

★ The average house has 30 spiders in it and you are never more than a metre away from a spider!

★ Spiders taste using their first pair of legs which have special hairs on them.

★ Spiders don't have mouths - they only drink liquid food which they make by injecting prey with special chemicals to liquify their insides!

Le chef-d'oeuvre
The masterpiece

Arty has made this picture so you can colour by letters. Can you remember all your colours?

BF = bleu foncé

BC = bleu clair

R = rose

O = orange

J = jaune

V = violet

M = marron

N = noir

GC = gris clair

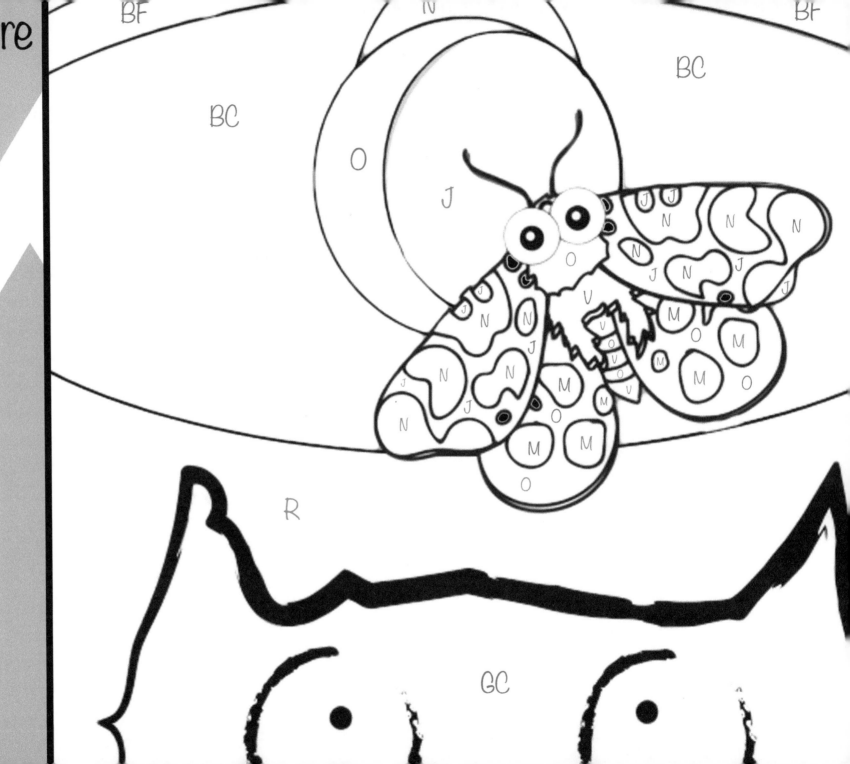

La fourmi

The ant

Find the two pictures of each insect that are the same size and colour them both.

Ant facts:

★ Ants can lift 50 times their own body weight!

★ Ants breathe through holes in their bodies.

★ Ants collect food by following scent trails. They have two stomachs: one for their own food, and one to store food to take back to the colony.

★ Most ants live in a nest but army ants move as a whole colony, eating everything in their path. They make a temporary camp every night.

★ Ants don't have ears, instead they can pick up vibrations through their legs to find out what is around them.

★ Ants communicate by secreting chemicals. An ant that has found food will leave a trail of chemicals on its way home, so that other ants can find the food source.

★ Queen ants can live for up to 26 years!

Create an insect

Two games to play

There are two ways to play this game. Firstly take a piece of paper and fold into three sections. Then take it in turns with some friends to draw the different parts of the insect. Each person only does one part and folds the paper so the others can't see what they have drawn. Unfold it at the end to see what you have created! For the second game, you choose a segment from the boxes below. Roll a dice three times for each segment and draw the parts the dice tells you. Be creative and make a unique insect!

Head	Thorax	Abdomen

Head	Thorax	Abdomen
1.antennae 2.horns 3.feelers 4.eyes 5.mandibles 6.tongue	1.legs 2.bumps 3.spikes 4.claws 5.ear holes 6.wings	1.spots 2.wing covers 3.segments 4.stinger 5. silk producer 6.hooks

Grossi à la loupe

Who can you see in each magnifying glass? Write the name in French and English on the card next to each one.

La libellule
The dragonfly

Dragonflies love water!

Colour the dragonfly in fantastic colours.

Water in the garden is very important for insects.
Draw insects and other things you might find
around a garden pond, into the picture.

Rotten log game

Be the first one to get to the centre of the rotten log, where the stag beetle can lay its eggs. But watch out! There is a lot of rotten wood in the log and you can easily fall out!

RULES:
Choose a counter and place it on the yellow square. Take it in turns to roll the dice. Move clockwise the number of places shown on the dice. Count in French. If you land on a green square you move in a ring. If you land on a red square move out a ring. If you move out of the log altogether, go back to the yellow start square. The black arrows show the direction to move. First one into the middle is the winner. Good luck!

le scarabée cerf

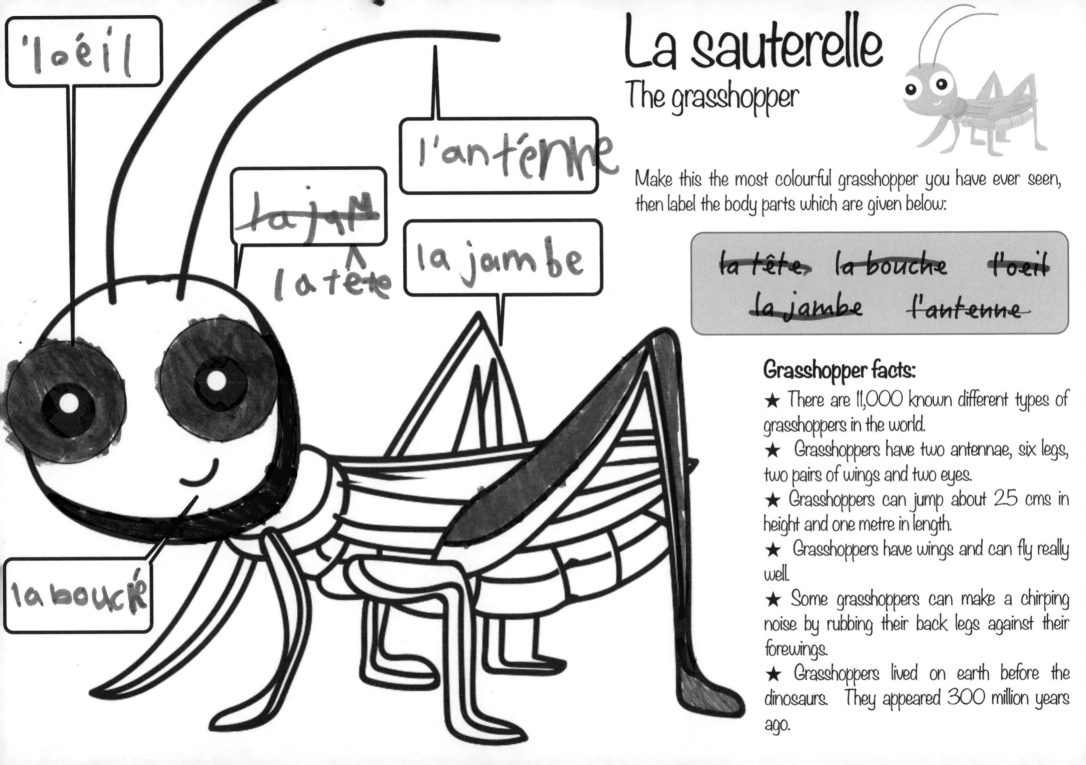

La sauterelle
The grasshopper

Make this the most colourful grasshopper you have ever seen, then label the body parts which are given below:

la tête   la bouche   l'oeil
la jambe   l'antenne

Grasshopper facts:

★ There are 11,000 known different types of grasshoppers in the world.

★ Grasshoppers have two antennae, six legs, two pairs of wings and two eyes.

★ Grasshoppers can jump about 25 cms in height and one metre in length.

★ Grasshoppers have wings and can fly really well.

★ Some grasshoppers can make a chirping noise by rubbing their back legs against their forewings.

★ Grasshoppers lived on earth before the dinosaurs. They appeared 300 million years ago.

'l'oéil

l'anténne

la jamb (crossed out)

la tête

la jambe

la tête

la bouche

Spot the difference

Arty is in the vegetable garden looking for insects. There are 15 differences between the pictures. Can you find them? Draw a circle around the differences on the bottom picture. We have done the first one for you. Good luck!

Use your magnifying glass to help!

Can you remember the French names of the insects?

L'abeille
The bee

Bee facts:

★ Honey bees live in large colonies of 40,000 bees. They build a honeycomb home from beeswax, and make and store honey.

★ There are three types of bee: a worker bee (female), a queen bee (female) and a drone (male).

★ Bees make beeswax from glands in their abdomens which they use to build their homes with. They build in hexagonal shapes.

★ Bees live from 1-3 months in the summer but up to nine months if they are surviving over winter.

★ The queen bee's job is to lay eggs. She lays up to 1,500 eggs a day!

★ Bumble bees live in smaller colonies of 50 but do not store honey over winter as only the queen survives. They have bigger, more hairy bodies.

★ Honey bees can only sting once and then die, but bumble bees can sting multiple times.

La guêpe
The wasp

Wasp facts:

★ Wasps differ physically from bees as they are not hairy, they have a very thin waist, have a louder buzz and are more brightly coloured.

★ Wasps make nests from paper. They take tiny strips of wood, chew them up and make a pulp which they build with.

★ A queen starts a new colony each spring. She raises a few workers first to make the nest and get food, and then she lays eggs to make the colony. Only the queen will survive over winter to start again.

★ Wasps eat other insects and lay their eggs in them so the babies have food when they hatch! They mostly eat insects that are pests but they do eat bees, nectar, tree sap and fruit! Wasps like human food, particularly fish sandwiches and fizzy drinks.

★ Wasps can sting multiple times, so take care if you see one and don't panic. They usually only sting to defend their nest, to subdue some prey or because they are in danger eg. they are about to be squashed or eaten!

★ A normal worker wasp only lives between 12-22 days! The queen can live for 12 months.

★ Wasps live in colonies of up to 13,000 individuals. A colony can produce 2,000 queens each year.

Dessine des ailes
Design the wings

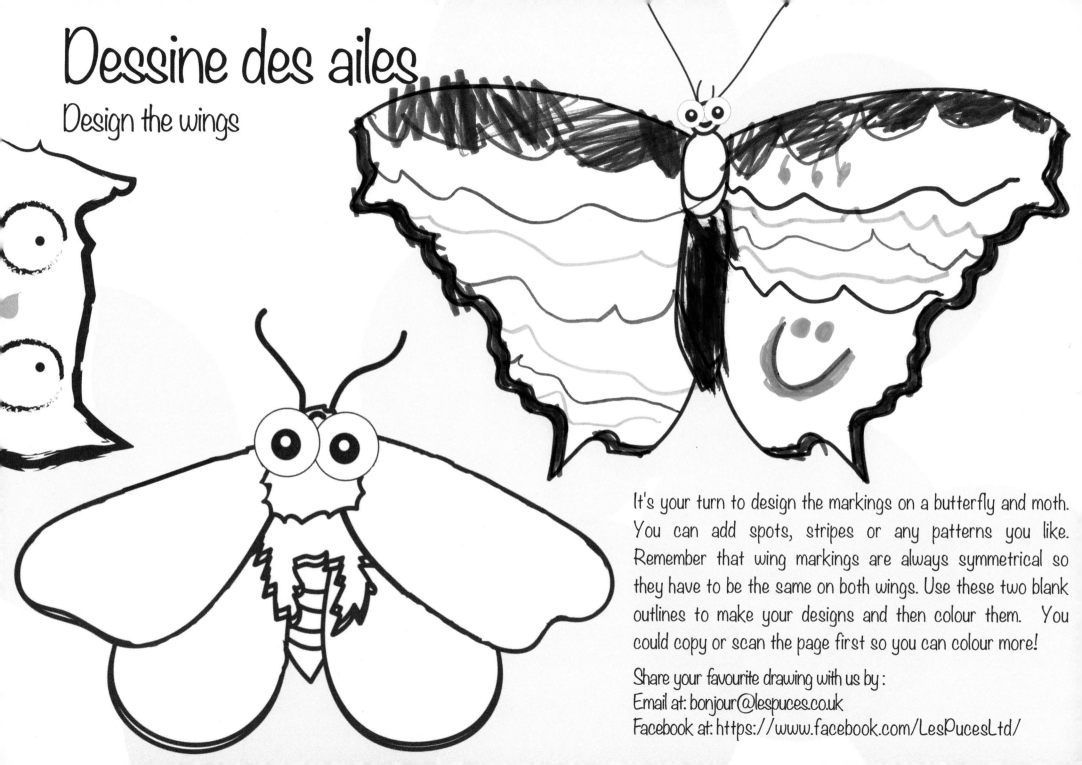

It's your turn to design the markings on a butterfly and moth. You can add spots, stripes or any patterns you like. Remember that wing markings are always symmetrical so they have to be the same on both wings. Use these two blank outlines to make your designs and then colour them. You could copy or scan the page first so you can colour more!

Share your favourite drawing with us by :
Email at: bonjour@lespuces.co.uk
Facebook at: https://www.facebook.com/LesPucesLtd/

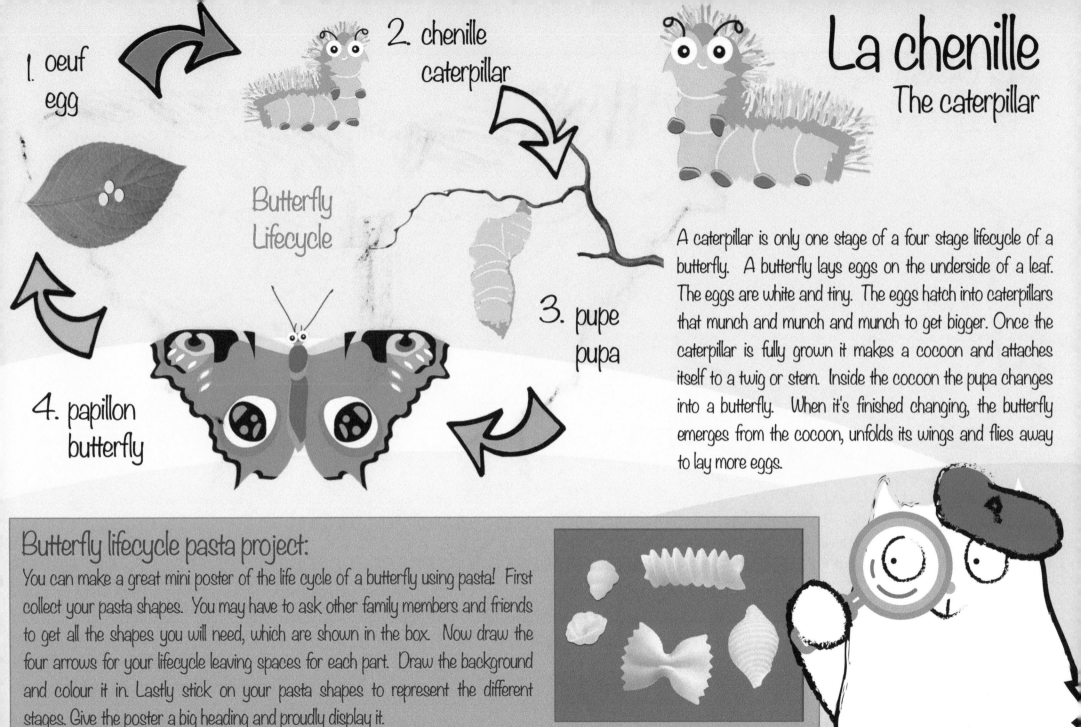

1. oeuf
egg

2. chenille
caterpillar

La chenille
The caterpillar

Butterfly
Lifecycle

3. pupe
pupa

4. papillon
butterfly

A caterpillar is only one stage of a four stage lifecycle of a butterfly. A butterfly lays eggs on the underside of a leaf. The eggs are white and tiny. The eggs hatch into caterpillars that munch and munch and munch to get bigger. Once the caterpillar is fully grown it makes a cocoon and attaches itself to a twig or stem. Inside the cocoon the pupa changes into a butterfly. When it's finished changing, the butterfly emerges from the cocoon, unfolds its wings and flies away to lay more eggs.

Butterfly lifecycle pasta project:

You can make a great mini poster of the life cycle of a butterfly using pasta! First collect your pasta shapes. You may have to ask other family members and friends to get all the shapes you will need, which are shown in the box. Now draw the four arrows for your lifecycle leaving spaces for each part. Draw the background and colour it in. Lastly stick on your pasta shapes to represent the different stages. Give the poster a big heading and proudly display it.

Le papillon de nuit

The moth

Use the squares to help copy the picture of the moth into the blank box and then colour it in. Can you make a really good copy?

Moth facts:

★ There are nine times more moths than butterflies in the world!

★ Most moths only come out at night, although some can live in the daylight.

★ Moths come in all sizes from a wingspan of 2 mms to that of the huge 30 cms Atlas moth!

★ Male moths have an amazing sense of smell and can find a female moth from 7 kms away!

★ Tiger moths can produce ultrasonic clicking noises to confuse bats so they don't get eaten!

★ To attract moths, mix up a moth cocktail of ripe banana, molasses and stale beer. Paint it on a tree trunk and see who turns up in the evening - just don't drink this cocktail yourself!

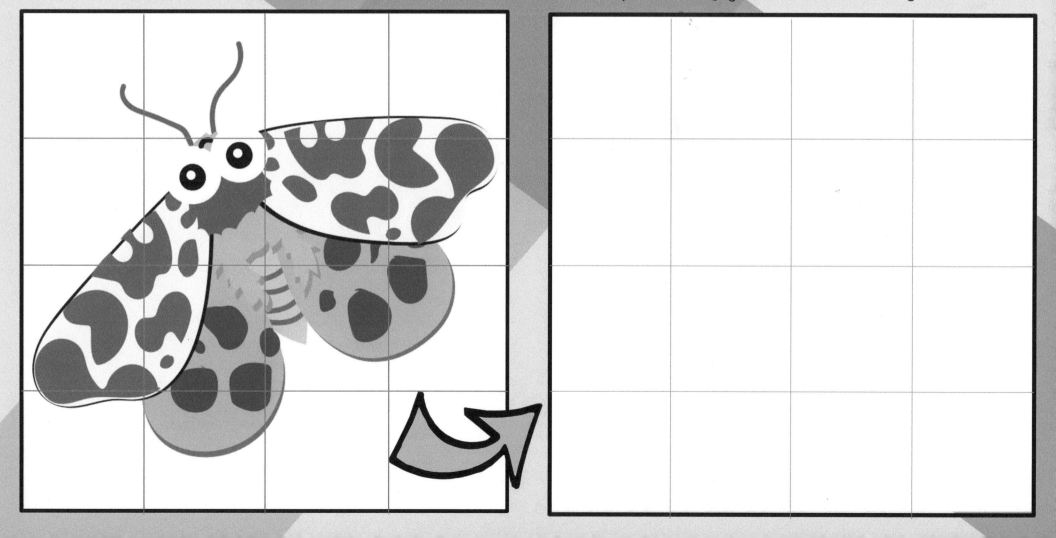

Trouve la différence !

Find the difference!

There are four pictures of each insect, but one of them is not the same! Circle the one that is different. You will have to look very carefully to find it. Can you remember the name of each insect?

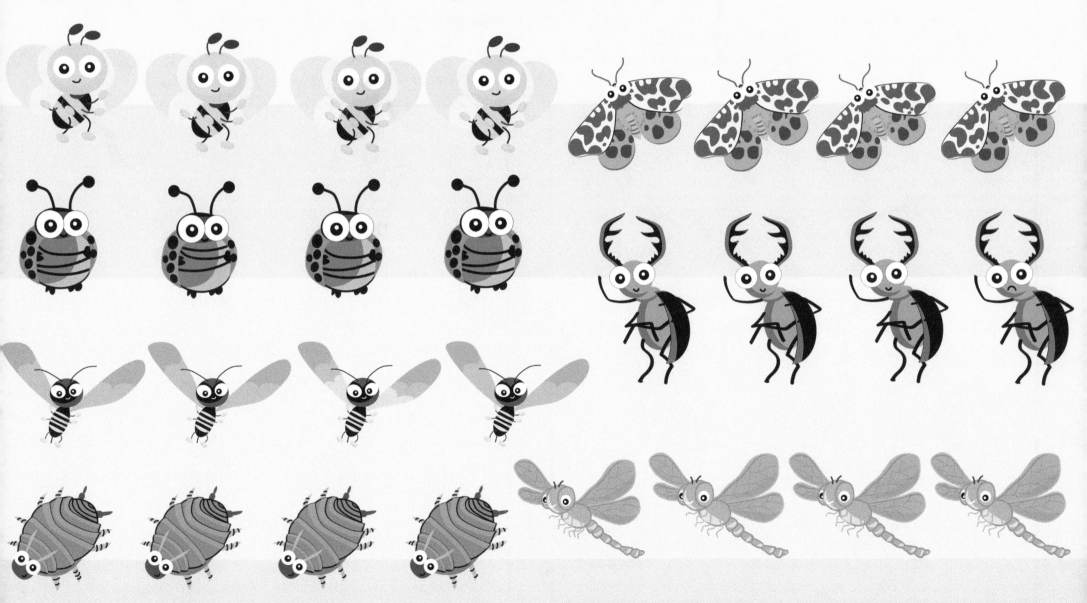

La coccinelle

The ladybird

Ladybird facts:

★ Ladybirds are a type of beetle. Some have up to 20 spots, some stripes and others none at all. They also come in different colours.

★ The ladybird has a bright shell to keep birds away as it acts as a warning that they don't taste nice!

★ If attacked, ladybirds can produce a smelly liquid from their back legs that deters predators.

★ Ladybirds live for up to one year. They hibernate in groups over winter. They come out when the temperature reaches $16°C$.

★ A ladybird can eat up to 5,000 aphids in its lifetime.

★ Ladybirds smell and taste with their antennae.

★ Ladybird lava are black and look like tiny alligators. They love eating aphids too.

★ Ladybirds can be male and female and all look roughly the same (unless you are a ladybird!).

Ladybird paper plate project:

1. Take two paper plates. Paint the back of one plate black, and the back of the other plate red.

2. Cut the red plate in half. These will be the ladybird's wings.

3. Cut out a circle of black card and glue to the black plate to make a head.

4. Use pipe cleaners or some curly card to make antennae. Draw or stick on eyes.

5. Use a split pin to secure the wings just behind the head so they can open up. Draw black dots on the wings.

6. Make a secret drawing, a special note or a heart shape. Open the wings and stick this to the middle of the black plate so that you can only see it when the wings are open!

Le scarabée cerf

The stag beetle

Stag beetle facts:

★ Stag beetles can grow up to eight cms long. They are the biggest beetles in the UK.

★ Stag beetles don't bite! Their huge jaws are used for wrestling other male stag beetles.

★ Female stag beetles are smaller and do not have big jaws, but can nip if handled.

★ Stag beetles can actually fly and you can see them flying on warm thundery evenings.

★ Stag beetle grubs eat rotting wood but the adults just drink sap and fruit juice with an orange tongue!

★ Stag beetles are an endangered species. You can help save them by making a rotting log pile in your garden to attract them.

★ Stag beetles live for 3-7 years as a grub but only 2-3 months as an adult.

Insect pebble painting project:

1. Find some nice smooth pebbles in the garden or out on a walk. If you take some from the beach just take a few please.

2. Wash your pebbles thoroughly with a good scrubbing and then dry them.

3. Use a permanent marker to lay out how you will paint your bug on the pebble.

4. You can paint them with acrylic paints, felt tip pens or chalk marker pens. Remember to let each layer dry before adding the next. You may want to varnish them when they are dry to stop the paint coming off. Now you can decorate your pot plants and garden with them.

Share your favourite pebbles with us by :
Email at: bonjour@lespuces.co.uk
Facebook at: https://www.facebook.com/LesPucesLtd/

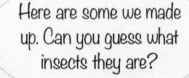

Here are some we made up. Can you guess what insects they are?

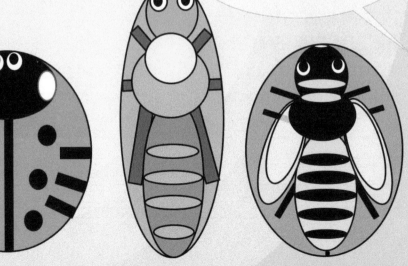

Mots croisés d'insectes

araignée
chenille
coccinelle
papillon
fourmi
guêpe
cloporte
abeille
tipule
sauterelle

DOWN
1. a long legged fly
2. big colourful wings
4. makes big jumps
7. makes honey
8. travels in long lines

ACROSS
3. black and yellow stripes
5. makes a web
6. small and prehistoric lookin
9. bright red with black spots
10. hairy and wriggly

Solve the crossword. The clues are in English and the answers in French. The names are on the page to help with spelling!

L'autre moitié

The other half

Finish the insect names by finding the other half of the insect and joining the two parts of the name together by filling in the spaces!

Perce- _ _ _ _ _ _ _ _

Gu _ _ _ _

Pun _ _ _ _ _

Clop*orte*i _l _l _e

Cocci _ _ _ _ _ _

Chen i _l _l _e

Arai _ _ _ _ _

Fou _ _ _ _

Scar _ _ _ _ _

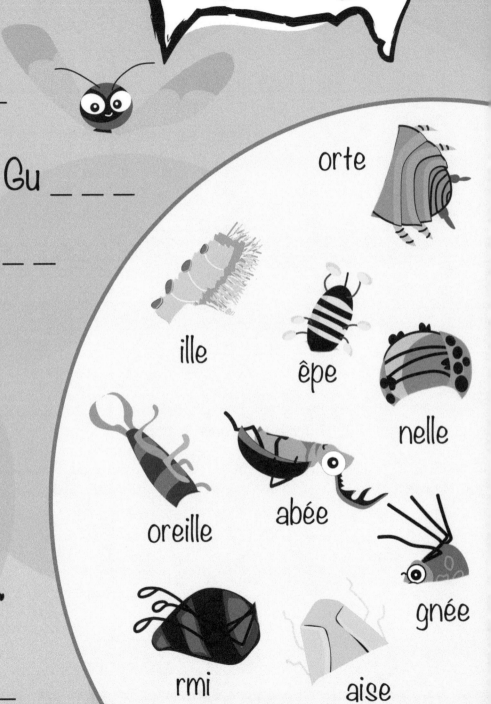

orte

ille

êpe

nelle

oreille

abée

rmi

aise

gnée

Insect wordsearch

The names of the insects are in French on the wordsearch. Words only go left to right and top to bottom. Draw a line around the word when you find it and put a circle around the insect picture below.

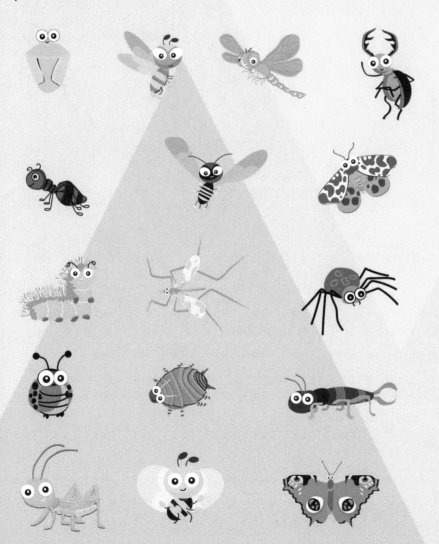

```
d o a p a p i l l o n - d e - n u i t h
t d c n j a l i b e l l u l e z a i c j
a f e u f g g y l q v c r w h e o j g l q
b n h a w o y e m j q u s y r p h e o i
e h t r r r j x s i c e s d f g f w p c
i g e a j r u c m r o v h m a p d e o o
l i d i b r w s r b f a e v e n i o r c
l m n g p e r c e - o r e i l l e z t c
e m h n t s v l p u n a i s e m y p e i
r g b é i y i w d d w w h g e u f t g n
b v h e p f f a h v f h c s j d m l u e
y v k r u o r p i s d l k v r a y d ê l
n d h u l u u d q q u z y k n d f d p l
s a u t e r e l l e u r u r e g t u e e
h c a n l m y k t r y a s c a r a b é e
a j w e r i g w v c h e n i l l e q w y
t w w k f b h x h s d o p q o j t u l v
d a c q h w m k t y y x p s r s r o z u
d c e v d r z g x t e s y g r c s q z w
c i f y a k b l j t p a p i l l o n r h
```

Mots brouillés

Scrambled words

S outérelle

lueaeletsr

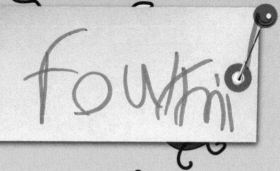
fourmi

imrouf

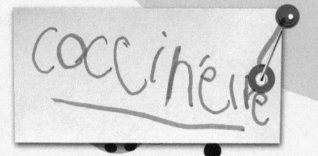
coccinelle

ioccclelne

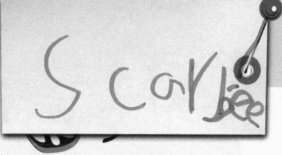
Scarabée

rbcasaeé

cloporte

rtpclooe

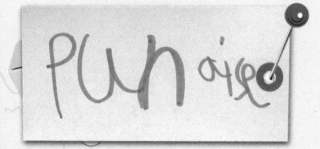
Punaise

aepisun

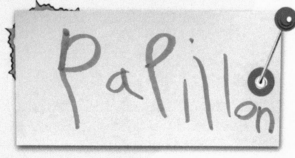
Papillon

nlpoapil

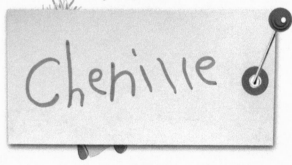
Chenille

ilcelhen

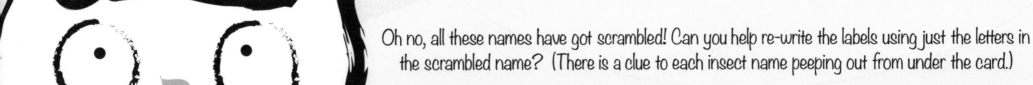
Oh no, all these names have got scrambled! Can you help re-write the labels using just the letters in the scrambled name? (There is a clue to each insect name peeping out from under the card.)

Find the butterfly!

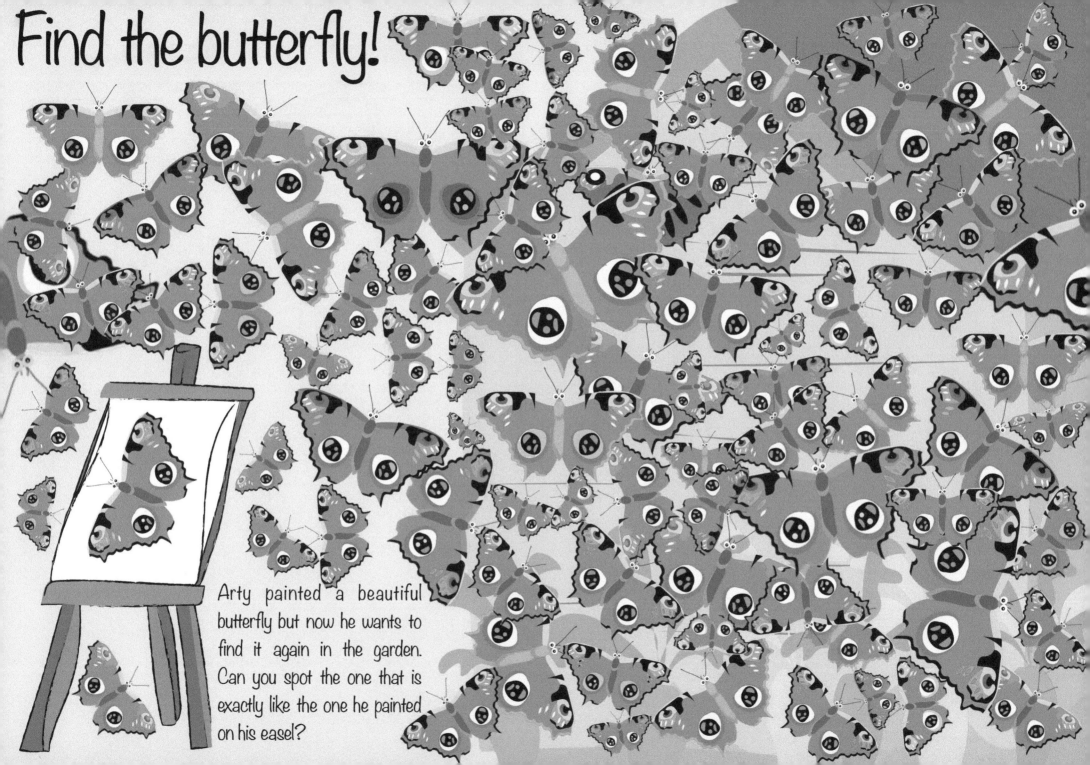

Arty painted a beautiful butterfly but now he wants to find it again in the garden. Can you spot the one that is exactly like the one he painted on his easel?

Le labyrinthe de fourmis

The ant maze

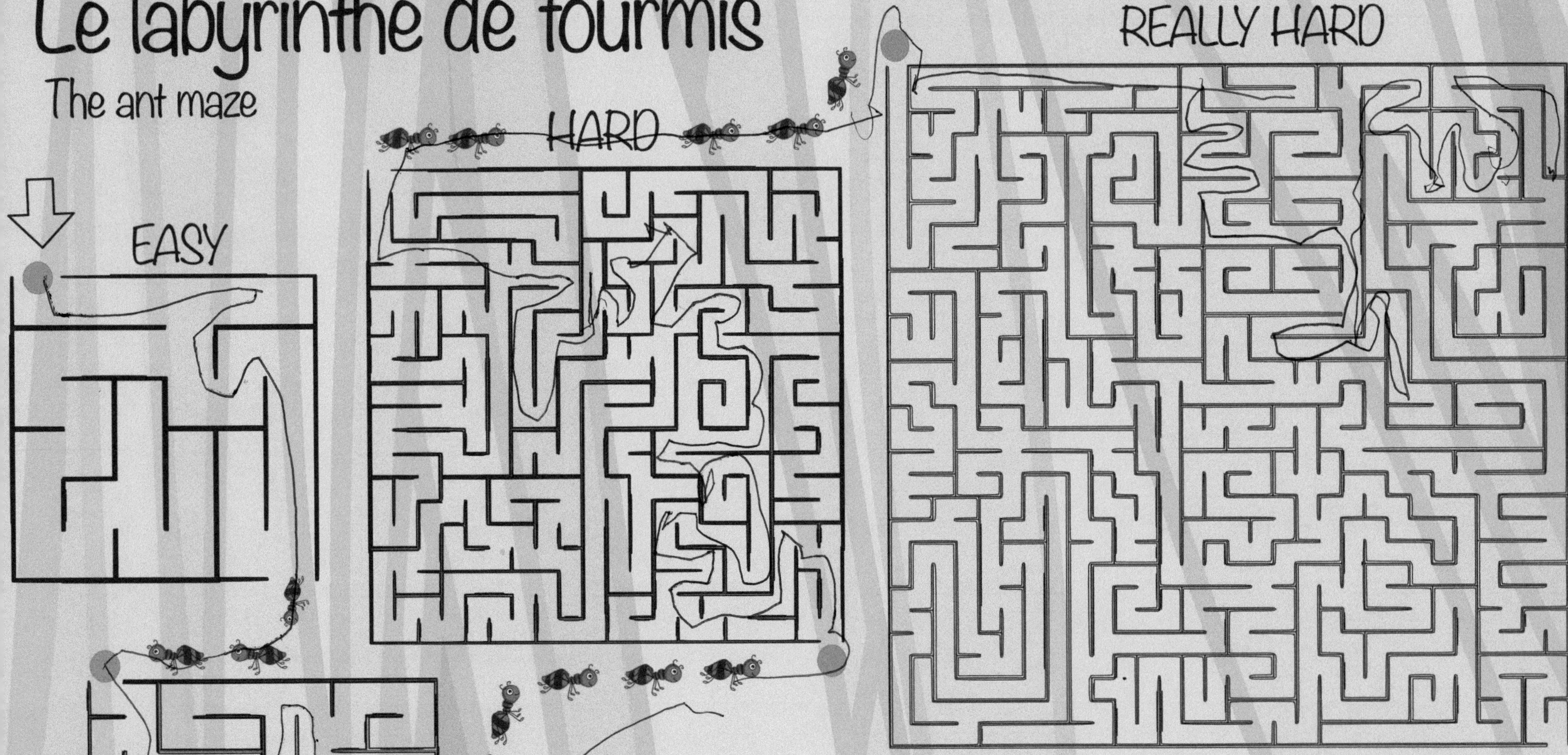

EASY

HARD

MEDIUM

REALLY HARD

SUGAR

SUGAR

SUGAR

Ants follow trails to find food and move around. Can you help the ants solve these mazes to get to the sugar? There are four mazes, each one more difficult than the next. You can't go on to the next maze until you have solved the one before!

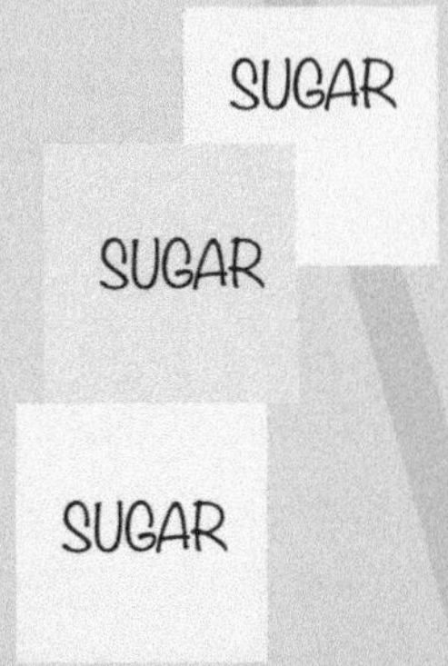

Build your own bug hotel project:

Place in a sheltered area away from wind near a hedge or wild garden.

Sturdy roof to keep eveything dry.

Who will move in?

Bamboo poles of different diameters stacked closely together.

Untreated wood blocks with different diameter holes drilled in them.

Dead wood branches with bark still on. Rolled up cardboard box. Dry dead leaves stuffed in tightly.

Sand clay, stones and earth mixed up and kept in with wire.

Keep off the ground to stop damp getting in.

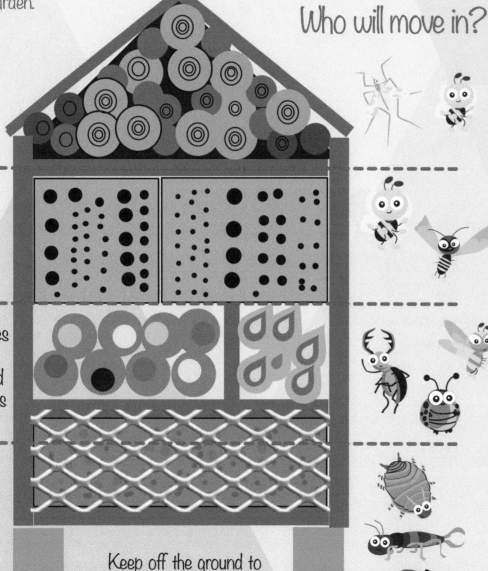

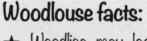

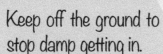

Le cloporte
The woodlouse

Woodlouse facts:

★ Woodlice may look like insects, but they are in fact crustaceans and related to crabs and lobsters!

★ They first appeared on earth about 360 million years ago!

★ Woodlice still breath through gills, as their ancestors used to live in water.

★ A woodlouse has 14 legs and an outer shell called an exoskeleton. To grow bigger it must moult its old exoskeleton. It does this in two parts - the front, and then back.

★ Woodlice eat rotting plants, fungi and their own poo! They live in damp dark places.

★ Female woodlice carry their eggs in a small pouch under their bodies. The young hatch out and stay in the pouch until they are big enough to survive on their own.

★ Woodlice live for 3-4 years.

★ There are possibly over 3,500 types of woodlice and about 35-40 types live in the UK.

The answers

Combien? ladybird - 8 bee - 18 butterfly - 3 dragonfly - 14 hoverfly - 7 moth - 12

La Coccinelle. Find the ladybirds: 1. - 3 2. - 4 3. - 11 4. - 10 5. - 2 6. - 5 7. - 8

Grossi à la loupe: 1. - ladybird/coccinelle 2. - shield bug/punaise 3. - earwig/cloporte 4. - grasshopper/sauterelle 5. - wasp/guêpe
6. - moth/papillon de nuit 7. - antler beetle/scarabée cerf

Trouve la différence: (counting from the left) Bee 3 - extra arm   Ladybird 2 - moved stripe   Wasp 3 - extra markings on wings
Woodlouse 1 - extra stripe on leg   Moth 3 - extra spot on white wings   Antler beetle 4 - smile   Dragonfly 1 - extra leg

Mots croisés d'insectes: 1. - tipule 2. - papillon 3. - guêpe 4. - sauterelle 5. - araignée 6. - cloporte
7. - abeille 8. - fourmi 9. - coccinelle 10. - chenille

The same size puzzle:

Spot the difference:

Insect wordsearch

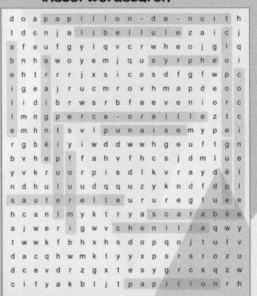

Find the butterfly

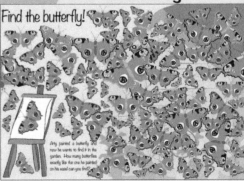

Find the butterfly!

Any painted a butterfly and now he wants to find it in the garden. How many butterflies exactly like the one he painted on his easel can you find?

Lightning Source UK Ltd.
Milton Keynes UK
UKHW051807280519

343468UK00004B/20/P